SPIRIT,
GOSPEL,
CULTURES

SPIRIT, GOSPEL, CULTURES

Bible Studies on the
Acts of the Apostles

MISSION
SERIES

WCC Publications, Geneva

Cover illustration: Icon of Pentecost, Mount Athos, Greece, presently at St Paul's Church, Chambésy, Switzerland.

Pentecost, the feast of the church in every age and every place, is the outpouring of the Holy Spirit, the "pledge of our inheritance" in Christ. The icon challenges an understanding of history that has no room for the mystery of salvation; it opens up the present by an eschatological vision. Note that Luke and Mark (evangelists) and Paul (apostle of the nations) are included among the twelve disciples — pointing to the unfolding fullness of God's saving purposes.

The icon also points to the fact that *all nations of the earth* are called to share in the blessings of the Spirit. The old person at the bottom of the icon (placed not in front of those who receive the Spirit but in their midst) represents "the cosmos". The world is not outside the church but in its very heart — and the church is an open, not closed, circle. The old person offers "the nations" to the church, with the conviction that the saints from all these nations will come, bringing their sufferings and struggles.

Scripture quotations are from the *New Revised Standard Version of the Bible*, copyright 1989 by the Division of Christian Education, National Council of the Churches of Christ in the USA. All rights reserved. Used by permission.

Also available in French, German, Spanish and Portuguese

Cover design: Edwin Hassink

ISBN 2-8254-1167-1

© 1995 WCC Publications, World Council of Churches,
150 route de Ferney, 1211 Geneva 2, Switzerland

No. 4 in the WCC Mission Series

Printed in Switzerland

Invitation

It is a privilege to present this set of Bible studies on the first seventeen chapters of the book of the Acts of the Apostles, and to invite you to explore how the gospel becomes enfleshed in a variety of cultures through the power of the Holy Spirit.

The studies have been specially prepared for reflection by the participants in the World Council of Churches' Conference on World Mission and Evangelism, to be held in Salvador, Bahia, Brazil, 24 November-3 December 1996, under the theme, "Called to One Hope — the Gospel in Diverse Cultures". The materials will also be useful to the growing number of local groups engaged in the WCC's gospel and cultures study process, which will inform the conference.

At the conference Christians from around the world will reflect on the inter-relationship of the gospel and cultures — a key concern in theology and mission today. They will explore questions such as how the gospel of Christ transforms human cultures, how culture shapes our response to the good news of the gospel, and how Christians may witness authentically in each cultural context.

We would like to invite you to participate in the preparation for this major mission event through prayer and study of the Acts of the Apostles from the particular perspective of the encounter between the gospel and cultures. Please feel free to share with us your reflections and insights. You are encouraged to translate these materials into your own language and make them available in every way possible to as wide a network as possible.

The Commission of the WCC's Programme Unit II commends these Bible studies to the churches in the hope that they will help equip the people of God for authentic witness in diverse cultures.

ANA LANGERAK
Executive Director, Programme Unit II
World Council of Churches

The Holy Spirit is light and life,
A living fountain of knowledge,
Spirit of wisdom,
Spirit of understanding,
Loving, righteous, filled with knowledge and power,
Cleansing our offences,
Divine, and making us divine;
Fire that comes forth from Fire,
Speaking, working, distributing gifts of grace.
By the Spirit were all the prophets, the apostles of God
    and the martyrs crowned.
Strange were the tidings, strange was the vision
    of Pentecost:
Fire came down, bestowing gifts of grace on each.

VESPERS OF PENTECOST, ORTHODOX

Table of Contents

God who is beyond our naming
and all our defining,
God from whose being flows creative diversity
and who is the source of our unity:
We worship you.

God who was born into the depths of our life,
who entered into our history in Christ,
facing the reality of every culture,
reflecting in every struggle for truth:
We worship you.

Spirit of God who dances free of us all,
calling us past boundaries
of race, gender, culture, system and nation:
We worship you.
We approach you in faith,
held fast by your love for the whole creation.

Introduction

This series of Bible studies has been written in preparation for the World Council of Churches' Conference on World Mission and Evangelism which will take place in Brazil in 1996. The conference will focus on issues related to the gospel in diverse cultures, seeking to understand the implications of a gospel that both challenges and is challenged by the cultures in which it finds itself, in order that churches and individual Christians may live and witness authentically in their own context. The conference is being preceded by a global study process on the inter-relation between the gospel and cultures.

The Acts of the Apostles is the second part of a two-volume work. The first volume, the gospel of Luke, is about "all that Jesus did and taught" (Acts 1:1). This second volume is a record of the witness of the disciples to Jesus Christ in many cultures. Both were written so that the church in every place and time and in diverse cultures might understand the gospel and learn from the life and witness of the earliest disciples. This is why the Commission of Programme Unit II — Churches in Mission: Health, Education, Witness — which bears the primary responsibility for organizing the world mission conference, considers a study of the Acts of the Apostles to be timely.

These studies have been designed to enable Christians to visit and dialogue with a single book of the Bible rather than with a few isolated passages from different books, selected to illustrate some of the points highlighted in the gospel and cultures study. It is important to bring our questions to the text and let the text in turn question us. There are other parts of the Bible which help us understand issues related to the gospel in diverse cultures; however, the Acts of the Apostles is considered to have more direct and greater relevance to this particular theme.

These studies deal with the first seventeen chapters of the book, in which (more than in the later ones) a variety of issues sharply arise out of the interaction of the gospel and cultures. The studies do not deal in the same detail with all the stories in the seventeen chapters. Rather, an attempt has been made to focus on particular passages within the larger context of the units of material surrounding them. For example, study 2 focuses on Acts 2:1-13 and 42-47 — but these texts are considered within the wider framework of chapters 2-4. It will no doubt be rewarding for those who use these studies to supplement this material by reference to other stories in Acts.

The book of the Acts of the Apostles cannot be taken as an objective recording or "orderly account" (Luke 1:3) of all the facts. Luke has selected and composed his materials to describe how the disciples bore their witness to the gospel "in Jerusalem, and in all Judea and Samaria, and to the ends of the earth" (Acts 1:8). He tells of how the church changed from being predominantly Jewish to becoming increasingly Gentile. The book was written also for the edification and encouragement of the churches, which at the time of writing (sometime between AD 70 and 100) were wrestling with persecution and with issues of division, class (rich and poor living in the same community), and so on. It is evangelical preaching aimed at building up the faith of the believers.

However, the witness of the apostles involves not only preaching. As disciples of Jesus, their witness is modelled on his. Following the way of Christ they preach, teach and heal in his name. Their witness to the reign of God is embodied also in communal life: "They devoted themselves to the apostles' teaching and fellowship, to the breaking of bread and the prayers... and had all things in common" (Acts 2:42,44). The gospel became enfleshed in all aspects of their daily life and culture.

It should be noted that the title "The Acts of the Apostles" was given long after the book was written — and does not really capture the fact that it is primarily about *the acts of Jesus through the Holy Spirit*. In the early church it is the Spirit who is the initiator of each step in the journey from Jerusalem "to the ends of the earth", and who unleashes powerful forces for change. The spread of the gospel is portrayed as the work of the Spirit rather than as the result of any planning or strategizing by the apostles. The spread of the gospel to other peoples and cultures is described as being the result of persecutions which scattered the believers as they sought to escape.

Furthermore, the book does not describe the acts of *all* the apostles, but focuses almost exclusively on those of Peter and Paul. It is concerned with the mission to the Gentiles and Paul's journeys ending in Rome.

The Acts of the Apostles betrays limits to Luke's interest, giving a particular bias to early church history which has influenced perceptions of and about the church ever since. For example, some have seen the book as having been written primarily in an appeal to the Roman authorities to recognize and respect the Christian religion in the empire. We wish it had described also the inculturation of the gospel in Alexandria, Ethiopia, other parts of North Africa and places east of Damascus. Furthermore, the concern for the whole inhabited world and the whole of life expressed in the first two chapters is not further developed.

It should also be noted that the Acts of the Apostles describes the relationship between the Jews and the early Christian community in a way that has led some Christians to understand that the Jews, in rejecting the gospel, have ceased to be people of God. Some also believe that Christians have supplanted the Jews as God's chosen people. In putting the blame for the death of Jesus on the Jews, the book has given rise to a negative attitude about Jews, contributing to centuries of rejection and persecution. It seems strangely arrogant for those who have been allowed gracious access to salvation in Christ to deny those with whom Christians are joint heirs their legitimate place in the plan of salvation (Rom. 11:17-20).

There is also the question of the place of women in Acts. The new community mirrored in the stories of the women and men who accompanied Jesus appears gradually to become a community in which the women seem almost peripheral to its life and witness. We wish that Luke had expanded his references to women. How did they bear their witness? Which house churches did they start and pastor? What happened to the women in Acts?

Notwithstanding, the Acts of the Apostles offers enriching vignettes of the ways in which the gospel was lived and proclaimed in diverse cultures in the early church.

These studies, prepared by a group of ten women and men from a variety of cultures and Christian traditions, are offered in the hope that churches, local groups and individuals will be stimulated to engage afresh with the Acts of the Apostles. The questions that different groups bring to the text, as well as the ways in which the text speaks to them, will vary from context to context.

It is hoped that those who engage in the studies will come to a face-to-face dialogue with the scriptures, through which Jesus Christ, the head of the church, calls each of us to faithful witness in our particular cultural context.

Suggestions for Bible Study Leaders

1. Ensure that all participants have *access to the material* — the biblical text (in their own language) and the study notes — either in written form or by retelling/rereading it.
2. Use the material *in your own way*. It is intended to stimulate and inspire, not to imprison or restrict. It is not necessary to use all the material. For instance, you may choose to use only one of the two passages suggested in studies 3 and 4.
3. You may wish to *supplement* this material by reference to other stories in Acts or elsewhere in the Bible.
4. Each study includes a few suggested *questions* — it is not necessary to deal with all of them, or to deal with them in order. Questions you may wish to keep in mind throughout include:
   - What questions do we bring to the text arising out of the way the gospel has come to us in our culture?
   - What questions does the text raise for us in our cultural situation?
5. Encourage the members of the group to *share their own stories* in response to the passage and the questions.
6. Find *imaginative ways* to respond to the Spirit and to articulate your reflections: silent meditation, prayer, drama, art, songs, poems, and so on.
7. It may be helpful for someone to keep a few *notes* on what you discover together.

In order to ensure full participation, you should make sure that everyone *knows* each other and hears a little of each other's background and reason for participating, and that everyone is able to *hear* and *see* each other.

Gracious God,
   by whose Spirit your people are led into all truth,
quicken within us an increasing love
   for the gospel of Jesus Christ
   as unfolded by the Spirit
      in the wondrous variety of human cultures.
Grant that, contemplating your glory
      in the bright mirror of your Word,
   we may be changed into that same image.
Speak to us this day,
   even as you spoke to your disciples,
that we too may awaken to your will
   and be alive to our part in witnessing to your love
      for the renewal of your whole creation.

STUDY 1

Acts 1

Focus: Acts 1:6-14

CALLED TO BE FAITHFUL WITNESSES
IN EVERY PLACE

Introduction

Acts 1 is the continuation of Luke's story of the promise of Jesus, the risen Lord: "You are witnesses of these things. And see, I am sending upon you what my Father promised; so stay here in the city until you have been clothed with power from on high" (Luke 24:48-49). The disciples are also told that they are to be "my witnesses in Jerusalem, in all Judea and Samaria, and to the ends of the earth" (Acts 1:8).

It is in *waiting* for the movement and power of the Spirit that the disciples will be empowered as Christ's witnesses. A strange call, to go and wait — at a time when the disciples were ready to join the Messiah in the hope that he would "restore the kingdom to Israel" (1:6).

It is also clear that the gospel will find its way to peoples and cultures in every part of the world not by the power of this small, fragile community but by the power and movement of the Holy Spirit. Similarly, the gospel is defined not by this community, but by "all that Jesus did and taught from the beginning" (1:1).

As disciples, their witness will be like that of Christ whom they serve. Its authenticity will be in how they embody the way of Christ in their personal and communal life (2:43-47) and in their preaching (2:14), teaching (2:42) and healing (3:6-7).

Commentary

6   For forty days after the resurrection of Jesus, his disciples impatiently await the realization of the promised kingdom. The apostles' question shows that they have not yet completely understood the nature of the reign of God. Probably

they thought about it only in categories of an earthly rule and expected its immediate beginning.

7   Jesus' answer implies that the date and time of the expected kingdom are completely in God's power, implemented not with human resources but by God. God as the creator of the world is in control of space and time.

8   The apostles are called to witness to the risen Lord through the power of the Holy Spirit, not through their own power.

9-11   Jesus' ascension is described in symbolic language drawn from the Old Testament (cf. 2 Kings 2:11, Dan. 7:13-14). The ascension is the completion of Christ's resurrection, symbolized by the figures of the "two men in white robes" (cf. Luke 24:4). Their words in v.11 may refer either to the second coming of Jesus (cf. 1 Thess. 4:16ff.) or to Pentecost, when the Spirit of the risen Lord will come upon the disciples.

12   The disciples return to Jerusalem from the Mount of Olives, which was "a sabbath day's journey" from Jerusalem, that is, approximately a kilometre — the distance a Jew was allowed to travel without violating the law of the sabbath rest.

13-14   The disciples wait in prayer for the promised Spirit, "together with certain women, including Mary the mother of Jesus, as well as his brothers". Women together with men form this earliest worshipping Christian community — a sign that all may participate in the gospel (cf. Luke 23:49 and 24:10-11).

The disciples hoped that the coming of the reign of God would mean the end of the oppressive domination of their land by the Romans. Like them, many people cry out daily to God for justice, for land, for respite... waiting for the kingdom.

A story: *WAITING FOR LAND*

The one who has no land has no power, is alone, without any strength.

This is one story of poor people in Latin America, in Indo-Afro-Latino-America. We are without any horizon, humiliated, with bowed head. We die of sorrow, of sorrow and hunger, as a plant which becomes dry without soil.

After so much suffering we decided to gather together. We prayed and sang. We read the Bible. We listened to the stories of others who are landless and went on our way towards land. At that moment we began to be in struggle.

We started travelling on the road. At Encruzilhada Natalina in the south of Brazil, our story took a new direction. On the roadside we built huts — some with pieces of wood, others with sheets of cardboard, in the desolate cold winter. We went to battle together with the whole family, with the children. To win or lose — it was all or nothing. Because hope grows only when we struggle hard. And it *was* hard: the winter, the rain, the cold, the sickness — everything was difficult. The police around, sometimes threatening us with clubs, sometimes offering candies to the children to confuse us. They wanted to extinguish our movement, our camp, our fight for land.

But they could not do it. Daily we prayed around the cross, read the Bible and organized concrete steps forward in our struggle for land.

And many supported us. They came from the cities to speak with us, sent clothes and food, came with us to demand our rights — our right for land to work. And we started getting our pieces of land...

Oh yes, it was worthwhile. If not alone, the poor have a chance.

But... until *when* should we have to wait for a life in dignity? Until *when* should we have to wait for a new culture, a culture of justice?

Questions

- Imagine that you are one of the disciples as the events in Acts 1 unfold around you. How do you feel? What response do these events evoke in you?

- What were the disciples hoping would happen (v.6)? For what do you and the people of your community yearn and cry out to God? What do you hope that the reign of God will bring to your community?

- What does it mean to be a witness in your own context? What for you is the equivalent of Jerusalem, Judea, Samaria and the ends of the earth?

O God, who on the day of Pentecost
    fulfilled your promise by pouring out your Spirit
        in flames of fire upon your disciples:
bestow upon your church in every race and nation
    the gifts of the same Spirit;
that through our living in the Spirit
    and witnessing to the gospel,
the knowledge and love of God
    may fill all peoples and cultures
        as the waters cover the sea.

STUDY 2

Acts 2-4

Focus: Acts 2:1-13, 42-47

THE SPIRIT AFFIRMS IDENTITY, CREATES COMMUNITY

Introduction

In Acts 2-4 we see the coming of the promised Holy Spirit and the empowerment of the disciples, Peter's explanation that this is a fulfilment of prophecy, and the beginnings of a new community. The new life is eventful (3:1-10, 4:23-31) and calls for the disciples' repeated witness to the risen Lord — cf. Peter in Solomon's Portico (3:11-26) and Peter and John before the council (4:1-22).

These chapters describe events which take place in Jerusalem, where the crucified Christ was raised from the dead in accordance with the scriptures. It is in Jerusalem, the seat of Israel's heritage, that the new community is born.

The fragile group of disciples has been told by Jesus to wait in Jerusalem: a treasured but ambiguous place where some see fulfilment and others find themselves excluded. Jerusalem is also significant as:

• a gathering place for "Jews from every nation" (2:5);
• the scene (at the time of Pentecost) of the Feast of Weeks or Feast of Harvest — a celebration of the beginning of the wheat harvest and one of the three pilgrimage feasts, which later came to be regarded as the concluding feast of Passover; it is also associated with the renewal of the covenant of Noah and Moses;
• a seat of regional government for Rome (cf. John 18:28);
• a place of hierarchy — the site of the temple, the architecture of which created order in rank (e.g., the court of the Gentiles, the court of the women).

It is precisely here that the Spirit of God chooses to encounter people in a new way.

Those who witnessed the experience and became caught up in it were astonished, as was Luke, who tried to describe and understand it. We too are astonished.

God is not creating a community with one colour and one flavour (like porridge or mealie-meal). The Spirit of God speaks through and to different people of quite different languages and backgrounds. Through emphasizing that each heard the gospel in his or her own language, Luke indicates that the identities of the hearers were affirmed. In the presence of the Spirit, difference need not mean division. No longer can any group or place or time claim to be more "sacred" than another.

Commentary

Acts 2:1-13

1	The Spirit comes to the disciples when they are "all together in one place". All are filled by the Spirit. Herein the beginning of a new community.
2-3	The Spirit in its coming is described as "a sound like the rush of a violent wind" (cf. Gen. 1:2, John 3:8). God is free to act where, when and with whom God chooses. God is not under human control. The rich symbolism which accompanies the coming of the Spirit is to be noted.
7	Those who are speaking are recognized as being Galileans — people from the poorer part of the country, generally looked down on as being rough and ill-educated. The people who had deserted their friend and teacher and had become dispirited and without hope, are now standing together to proclaim his story (cf. Ezek. 37:11-14). The Spirit brings these peripheral Galileans to the centre stage of the resurrection story. In the Spirit affirming their identity, a sign of God's new age is made manifest.
8-11	The people hear, each in his or her own language, the disciples speaking about God's deeds of power. Luke's enumeration of the crowd indicates that it is made up of Jews, proselytes (converts to Judaism) and others from different ethnic groups all over the biblical world. A variety

of cultures is being addressed and thereby affirmed (contrast with Gen. 11:1-9).

Acts 2:42-47 (see also 4:32-37)

This passage describes the life and growth of the community (see vv.41 and 47) formed by the power of the Spirit.

42   These are basic expressions of Christian life in community.

43-45   The transforming presence of the Spirit of God brings about "wonders and signs" for all to observe, as well as transformed lives: those who believed "had all things in common" — witness in *being* and *doing*. The sharing of material goods, so that "there was not a needy person among them" (v.34), is an essential dimension of community in the Spirit. The believers are not selfish or possessive with what they own but are ready even to sell their property for the common good — thus expressing the purposes of God for a new human community.

46   Life in the Spirit is not confined to the temple. In addition to spending time together in prayer in the temple, they gather in homes to praise God and break bread — a central sign of their communion with the risen Lord and with each other.

A story: *A MOMENT OF PENTECOST*

In May 1993 a group of three hundred youth gathered in Kansas City, Missouri, USA, hosted by two inner-city churches. They came from many parts of the country and from different cultures and religious understandings. They were Latino, Native American, African American, young men and young women. They were Christians, Muslims, black Hebrews, people of traditional native religions. They were Crips, Bloods, Disciples — gangs that saw each other as enemies, creating a culture of death. But in these days they came to choose life over death, friendship over enmity.

For three days they laboured and struggled to strategize and envision a new future living together, respecting and affirming each other's identity. There were volatile moments when conflict arose, but each time they prayed and waited until they could hear each other and understand in their own cultural language. Some prayed in the name of Jesus; others prayed in the name of Allah or Jehovah. At each of the moments of decision, as we waited we could feel the power of the Spirit moving, allowing us to hear one another, creating new community. During the three days we ate together, prayed together, danced together and worshipped together.

The Christian community shared its resources to enable this moment of Pentecost to happen. All were transformed as the Holy Spirit enabled us to hear and see each other anew.

> *Living youth in the streets*
>   *killing one another over colours*
>   *gang colours*
> *robbing, raping, handling guns*
>   *and drugs — surviving*
>   *hopeless*
> *turning inward — killing*
>   *killing all who differ*
> *speaking the language of division*
>   *and hate and hurt*
>   *marginalized   excluded   frightened*
>   *seeking   turning   calling   crying*
> *crying to be heard   loved   seen*
>   *and listening...*

Spirit of the risen Christ,
as your disciples were bound together in the bond of peace
and built up into one body as they broke bread
and remained in prayer:
so set your blessing upon the fellowship we share
      in Jesus' name.
Renew our common life
      through your Word and sacraments,
that we may awaken to your will for us
      and be alive to our part in your work in the world,
            to the glory of your Triune name.

Questions

- At Pentecost the Spirit affirmed the identity of each group and yet bound them together in a single community. What are the consequences of affirming identities at the expense of community, or of affirming community at the expense of identities?

- What are the marks of a Spirit-filled community as seen in Acts 2-4? What are signs of the presence of the Spirit in your community?

- Identify an instance where, through the power of the Spirit, diverse ethnic, racial, language, religious or other groups were brought together in a common cause.

- What are the ways in which a local congregation/parish can be a sign of God's inclusive love across cultural, class or other divides?

Acts 5-7

Focus: Acts 5:27-32, 6:1-7

THE GOSPEL CHALLENGES SOCIETAL STRUCTURES AND THE NEW COMMUNITY

Introduction

These chapters help us to see ways in which the gospel poses hard questions to different groups. The gospel addresses itself to power relationships in society, and the early Christian community also has to struggle with various internal tensions which threaten its unity.

It is clear from the choice of stories in chapters 5-7 that Luke does not want to portray an idealistic view of life in the infant Christian community. The struggles and challenges facing that community are real and testing.

Luke ended the previous chapter with a powerful description of the communal life of the believers. At the very beginning of chapter 5, however, that corporate life is threatened when two members of the community withhold part of the proceeds of the sale of a piece of land — and then lie about it. The consequence of those actions is death.

The Spirit continues to work "many signs and wonders" through the apostles. This provokes the antagonism of the Jewish authorities, and various attempts (including imprisonment) are made to prevent the apostles from teaching in the name of Jesus. In these encounters with the religious authorities, the Spirit empowers the apostles to be faithful to the gospel and to continue their witness.

In chapter 6, Luke shows how the community deals with the pressures and tensions amongst themselves. Two groups — Hellenists (Greek-speaking Jews) and Hebrews (Jews who spoke Hebrew or, more probably, Aramaic) — try to find ways of organizing their communal life so that all may have access to the resources available, leaving the apostles free to continue their ministry unhindered.

Luke then describes the conflict with the authorities, relating the story of Stephen's preaching and martyrdom. It is clear that the actions and words of Stephen, who is described as being "full of grace and power" (6:8), were a great irritant to the Greek-speaking Jews in one particular synagogue, who "could not withstand the wisdom and the Spirit with which he spoke" (6:10).

Arrested and brought before the council, Stephen speaks in the power of the Spirit concerning the history of God's ways and works with the people of Israel and the fulfilment of God's promises. His address makes explicit the judgment of God upon those who oppose the Holy Spirit (7:51-53). As his hearers become enraged, Stephen is sustained by a vision of Jesus standing at the right hand of God. His last prayer, like his Lord's, is for forgiveness for those who were putting him to death. Luke is careful to mention Saul's approval of the stoning.

Everyone's life, it seems, will be turned upside down by the presence and acts of the Spirit. We are left with the question: how can we be open to the uncomfortable challenge of the gospel as we bear prophetic witness and reorder our communal life according to the promptings of the Spirit?

Commentary

Acts 5:27-32

27   The bold proclamation of Peter and John immediately after their release from prison (5:19-21) angers the authorities, whose control over the ordering of society is being threatened. By quoting from Psalm 2 in Acts 4:25-26, Luke indicates that the church should not be surprised at this kind of response by the authorities.

28   The perplexity and anger of the authorities is predictable due to the breaching of their order to remain silent. They fear that the apostles' teaching will "bring this man's blood on us". Does not the gospel often create a sense of insecurity amongst those who are not accustomed to having their authority questioned?

29   The gospel demands that the apostles make a radical choice: to obey God or to obey a human authority (cf. Luke 16:13).

30   The apostles' choice leads them to unequivocal witness to God's raising of Jesus from the dead. It is that act of God which becomes judgment upon those who killed Jesus.

31   God's exalting of Jesus as "Leader and Saviour" makes repentance and forgiveness available to Israel, including those who hear the apostles speak. The human response to God's offer, however, is frequently one of rebellion and rejection (cf. v. 33). Often those in positions of power and privilege find it particularly difficult to respond to the gospel.

32   The witness of the disciples is inspired and sustained by the Holy Spirit, in accordance with Jesus' promise to them before his ascension (1:8). In speaking of themselves in the present tense — "we *are* witnesses" — the apostles affirm the very purpose of their being.

Loving God, source of renewal,
    open to us your new life.
Enable us as your community of faith
    to risk living the way of Jesus.
Help us to put aside our love of security
    and to enter the new life of the Spirit.
Show us the way of Jesus,
    the way to bring about justice and peace in the world.

Acts 6:1-7

1   As the early Christian community grows, the diversity within that community becomes increasingly problematic. Despite their common faith in the risen Lord, the disciples are faced with tensions in their day-to-day life. A familiar kind of complaint surfaces: the Hebrews were neglecting the Hellenist widows in the daily distribution of food. The complaint is made on behalf of those who were poor and undoubtedly in the minority.

2   It is important to note that the *whole* community is called together to discuss the issue. The apostles feel that the responsibilities should be shared so that they may be free to devote themselves to prayer and the proclamation of the gospel (v.4). Delegation of tasks and sharing of respon-

sibilities are essential for the smooth functioning of communal life.

3   It is the whole community who chooses the seven. The method of choosing is different from that used to replace Judas with Matthias at the beginning of Acts (1:26): here the community exercises *discernment* in the Spirit. Those chosen are to be "of good standing, full of the Spirit and of wisdom".

5   All seven have Greek names. Their appointment demonstrates sensitivity in relation to the situation of neglect which had led to breakdown in the life of the community.

6   Those who have been appointed to serve the community are set apart and commissioned (cf. Moses' appointment of "heads over the people" to help in administration, Ex. 18:17-26), through the laying on of hands. Thus the Holy Spirit enables the early Christian community to meet an internal threat to its communion.

7   Before turning to the story of Stephen's martyrdom, Luke reminds us that the early Christian community continues to grow and that many people, including priests, come to believe. The challenge of the gospel is lived in and through a fragile and vulnerable community.

Spirit of unity,
    reconcile your people.
Give us the wisdom
    to hold to what we need
    to be your church.
Give us the grace
    to lay down
    those things that we can do without.
Give us a vision of your breadth and length and height
    which will challenge our smallness of heart
    and bring us humbly together.

A story: *A PROPHETIC STANCE*

In Kenya there are two dominant tribes, Kikuyu and Luo. Since independence in 1963 both tribes have wanted the leaders of the country to come from them.

The first president, the late Jomo Kenyatta, was a Kikuyu. When he became old he wanted a Kikuyu to take his position — whereas the Luo believed it was their turn. This caused division between the two tribes. To unify the Kikuyu people, an oath-taking ceremony was established for them in 1969. Some Kikuyu Christians (many of them from urban areas) refused to take the oath because of their Christian principles: they said they would never fight their Luo compatriots. This caused chaos in the country, especially when many Kikuyu believers were martyred.

This forced the Anglican, Methodist and Presbyterian churches to work together. They found the courage to visit the president to talk about this issue. Following this confrontation with the head of state, it was agreed that the oath-taking ceremony would henceforth be administered only to those who chose to participate in it. The meeting of these heads of churches with the president showed how a problem can be solved through discussion. When people speak with one voice they are better able to solve problems. It is important for the church to take a prophetic stance in the face of injustice and wrong.

Questions

- In the light of Acts 5:29, how may resistance be a form of witness?

- How can insights from Acts 6:1-7 contribute to equity, participation and just sharing in community?

- What are some of the causes of division in your congregation/church today, and how does the gospel help you to address them?

- What aspects of your community life may be contrary to the values of the gospel?

Acts 8-9

Focus: Acts 8:26-40, 9:1-19

THE GOSPEL TRANSFORMS PERSONS
AND CULTURES

Introduction

Seeds, once scattered and sown in the ground, are transformed: they germinate, grow up and spread. This is what happens in the early Christian community in Acts 8-9.

The spreading, however, involves suffering and death (cf. John 12:24-25). One of the disciples, Stephen, was martyred (Acts 7:54-60), and the persecution from the authorities was severe (8:1-3).

Luke's narrative indicates that the Christian community often grows through persecution of the believers. As Tertullian later wrote: "The blood of the martyrs is the seed of the church."

Seeds scattered and sown are seeds that come to life and spread. This life continues through Philip (8:5). It spreads through Samaria (8:4-25), south to Ethiopia (8:26-39) and north to Damascus (9:22). The gospel of abundant life will spread to Lydda and Joppa (9:32-43) and into other lands (ch. 10). Its transforming power is experienced in ever-widening circles.

Philip, and later Peter and John (8:14-25), are bearers of the good news of change in Samaria. A former magician, Simon, becomes astonished at the miracles worked by Philip and is baptized. When he sees that "the Spirit was given through the laying on of the apostles' hands", he offers them money to give him this power. But God's gift cannot be obtained with money.

Philip then goes to meet the Ethiopian eunuch (8:26-40), a high government official in charge of the queen's treasury. The eunuch (who has power and wealth) is reading the suffering servant passage in Isaiah — without understanding it. After Philip's explanation, the Ethiopian is enlightened and transformed.

Saul goes to Damascus armed with power to arrest "any who belonged to the Way" (9:2). In his encounter with Christ he becomes powerless, defenceless. Transformed by the Spirit, he is integrated into the Christian community and becomes a powerful witness to the risen Lord.

In these chapters the focus is on the transforming power of the gospel in the lives of the Ethiopian eunuch and of Saul.

Commentary

Acts 8:26-40

26   Philip receives divine instruction to undertake this journey.

27-28   The eunuch, a court official in charge of the treasury of the Candace, the queen of the Ethiopians, was returning home by chariot from a pilgrimage to Jerusalem. ("Candace" is a dynastic name, like Pharaoh or Caesar, borne by the queens and queen mothers of southern Nubia in Ethiopia; it should be noted that this is one of the few references in the Bible to a woman with power and authority.)

29   Philip again responds to the prompting of the Spirit by going over to the chariot, where he hears the man reading the passage in Isaiah (53:7-8) about the suffering servant. (It was extraordinary for an individual to have access to a scroll of the scriptures; scrolls at that time were precious and rare.)

30-35   On being invited to join the eunuch in the chariot, Philip, beginning with this scriptural text, proclaims to him the good news about Jesus (cf. Luke 24:27, 44-45).

36-38   Coming to some water, the eunuch asks: "What is to prevent me from being baptized?" Though eunuchs were excluded from public worship (Deut. 23:1), Philip baptizes him into the community of believers. (Perhaps Luke has in mind Isaiah 56:3-8, where eunuchs and foreigners are included in the people of God.)

39   Transformed by the power of the Spirit, the Ethiopian continues on his way rejoicing. His witness would later make an impact on his people and their culture. Herein our attention is drawn to the outreach of the gospel to the nations.

God, who gave your Son Jesus Christ
    as the measure of your immeasurable love,
gather your people from every tribe, language and nation
    into your eternal kingdom.
How great it will be, when bound together in love,
    we worship you in all our languages
    in songs of never-ending praise.
Alleluia!

Acts 9:1-19 (see also 22:3-21, 26:2-23)

1-2   The merciless persecutor Saul (a Greek-speaking Jew with Roman citizenship as well, who had studied the law under Gamaliel in Jerusalem, outstripping his contemporaries in zeal for the traditions of the past — cf. Gal. 1:14) is on his way to Damascus with letters of authority from the high priest to identify and arrest men and women who "belonged to the Way".

3-5   Saul believed that in persecuting the Christians he was serving God. On the road to Damascus he hears a voice saying, "Saul, Saul, why do you persecute me?" Saul discovers that the one who died a hideous death on the cross is the Lord, and that it is *the Lord* whom he has been persecuting! This recognition is life-transforming indeed.

6   Saul learns only that he will be told what he is to do. His life of obedience begins.

7-9   The overwhelming revelation exposes the false foundations on which Saul's life has been based. His companions on the journey are speechless, and as for Saul, "though his eyes were open, he could see nothing".

11-16   Ananias is instructed in a vision to minister to Saul, but is reluctant to have anything to do with the known persecutor. But the Lord tells him that Saul has been "chosen to bring my name before Gentiles and kings and before the people of Israel".

17-19   Ananias is now able to greet Saul as a brother and to minister to him. Laying his hands on Saul, he helps him recognize that the one who sent him is the same Lord Jesus who had met Saul on the road to Damascus, and that the purpose of the encounter is for Saul to be filled with the Holy Spirit. At the moment of recognition, Saul regains his sight. The transformed Saul is now baptized, takes food, and comes into communion with the disciples. The gospel has transformed a persecutor into a herald of that same gospel.

A story: *A TRANSFORMING VISION*

Metropolitan Anthony Bloom is one of the best-known bishops in the Russian Orthodox Church. He lives in London and is an old man now. He was born into a Russian family, but in his childhood his family was forced to move abroad, first to France and then to Britain. As a young man (like many people of his age in the 1920s) he had no religious beliefs. He refused to go to religious education classes at school, derided the Holy Scriptures and made fun of his devout relatives and acquaintances. He was, however, an honest young man. One day he was told that he should not mock something he did not even know, and so he decided to read the gospel. He began with the gospel of Matthew but quickly decided that it was too long and boring, and so started to read the shortest account, the gospel of Mark. He was reading it one evening in his dark room by the light of a table lamp, not noticing how quickly the time passed. Suddenly he clearly felt that there was someone else in the room. Jesus was standing next to him. His presence was so real that the young man's doubts were cast away: Jesus lives!

This sense of the presence of Jesus has been with Anthony until now. The encounter happened at a time when a new, false, pseudo-religion was being preached in his home country. Propaganda and the mass media repeated every day: Lenin lived, Lenin lives, Lenin shall live! — a blasphemous parody of the Christian belief in the living Christ. Thousands of people paid tribute in the Moscow mausoleum, the communist temple, to the preserved body of Lenin.

Anthony Bloom decided that henceforth whatever he would do would be done in the name of Jesus. First he studied medicine and became a heart surgeon. During the second world war he joined the French resistance movement fighting the Nazis. After the war, in accordance with a call from Christ, he became a monk. Many years later he was made a bishop. He received the great gift of preaching, and published his sermons, which every week were broadcast by the BBC and heard by many in Britain and the USSR. In the USSR his books were prohibited. But his voice proclaiming the gospel of Jesus Christ led to the conversion of many, convincing them to turn to God.

For many in the USSR, the missionary activity of Metropolitan Anthony was as vital as water for someone dying of thirst in the desert. This man not only fulfils his apostolic duty; he was and is a bridge between peoples, cultures, languages and confessions.

Questions

- Consider Philip's openness to the guidance of the Spirit, without knowing the consequences. How is the experience of being led by the Spirit related to organizing and strategizing for mission?

- Saul persecuted the Christians on the basis of his religious convictions. What are some of the ways in which people of faith today can be blinded to the truth by their religious/cultural preconceptions?

- Give an illustration of how different aspects of your culture have enabled you to understand the gospel in a fresh way.

God, you often take us by surprise;
you do not tell us your name.
You make yourself known to us
   in the events that happen along the way.

God, give us the courage to take risks
   to build a highway in the desert
   when we do not see
   how we can possibly move forward.
Give us courage to believe that you are there,
   and will be ahead of us when we dare to move.
Give us courage to believe that we as a church
   will find you there,
   to honour the things we dare to do,
   when we are prepared to take the risk
   and carry the first rock to build the highway.

Acts 10-12

Focus: Acts 10:1-48

MUTUAL MISSION — MUTUAL CHANGE

Introduction

The Holy Spirit continues to guide the early Christian community, helping it to a deeper understanding of mission. In every encounter the Spirit reveals to the community something new. In Acts 10:1-48, where the focus is on the encounter between Peter and Cornelius, the newness is in the learning that "God shows no partiality" (10:34), leading to an understanding of God's inclusive love and of mutuality in mission.

Cornelius was a God-fearing centurion who longed for a deeper understanding of the ways and works of God. Guided by the Holy Spirit, Peter visits Cornelius — and through this encounter both are changed.

In the course of the encounter the Spirit surprises them both, freeing especially Peter from previous preconceptions. Both are enriched and mission becomes mutual. The Spirit continues to work in and through us as we meet others and are met by them, giving and receiving, teaching and being taught, understanding and being understood. The evangelist is also evangelized.

In earlier chapters we met Peter through his activities (3:1-10, 5:12-16, 8:14-25) and especially through his speeches (2:14-36, 3:12-26, 4:8-12), which cover a wide range of issues and include many of the indispensable elements of the Christian faith. Some of the speeches are polemical (to resolve controversy), while others are a reasoned defence of the Christian faith, with an element of exhortation to repentance and belief.

In 9:32-43, Peter visited the Hellenistic cities of Palestine, where he proclaimed the good news and worked miracles of healing. It was the death of a woman named Tabitha (in Aramaic) or Dorcas (in Greek) — the only woman in the Acts of the Apostles called "a disciple" — which brought Peter from Lydda to Joppa.

Chapters 10-12 describe Peter's crucial role in spreading the gospel to the Gentiles, preparing the way for their acceptance into the early Christian community.

Commentary

Acts 10:1-48

1-3	Cornelius is described as being someone who had a knowledge of and relationship with God even before Peter brings the gospel to him. This "devout man who feared God... and prayed constantly to God" (v.2) is, however, called to a deeper encounter with God.
4	The passage affirms that the prayers and alms of *a Gentile* "have ascended as a memorial before God".
7-8	In the biblical narratives the encounter with God is often followed by an active response in faith.
9-16	Peter, a devout Jew who thought he knew the meaning of faithful life, is confronted by God with a new dimension of obedience in mission. He sees a vision in which he is told to eat meat which according to Jewish law was ritually unclean. The fact that the vision had to be repeated three times points to how religious convictions can sometimes hinder people from opening themselves to the call of the Spirit and to new learning.

In these two passages (1-8 and 9-16), the Spirit leads both men into a new encounter.

19-20	The same Spirit which has prepared and freed Peter to move forward now leads him into a new frontier of mission.
21-22	Both men send for/visit and receive each other only in response to God's command and not with any clear knowledge of what will transpire (cf. v.29).
23-29	One cannot deny the courage of both men in undertaking these visits, it being strictly forbidden for Jews to have as a guest or be the guest of anyone who did not observe the law. God's revelation that what God has made clean no one must call profane, abrogates that which has been "unlawful for a Jew". Further, it appears that Peter went to see

Cornelius in direct response to the Spirit, not because he is following a clear mission strategy.

30-33   The mission that started with an opening of one's self to a new reality, continues by accepting to be with the other, despite the differences. Through the Spirit, Cornelius is now open to the presence of God and to "all that the Lord has commanded you to say".

34-43   Peter's testimony begins with a confession of his own new understanding that "God shows no partiality" and is access-ible to all peoples.

The ministry of the word in Peter's sermon was preceded by an action of acceptance of others, their culture and practices. Peter not only ministers to Cornelius, but is ministered to. Peter's ministry also includes an unequivocal witness to God's decisive act in Jesus Christ and the offer of forgiveness of sins through his name.

In v.41, Peter points to the fact that the disciples' experience of and witness to the risen Lord is intrinsically linked with the memory of Jesus' table fellowship, their eating and drinking with him.

44-48   When all are open to the Spirit, astounding things take place. Even before Peter has finished speaking, before anyone could be baptized, the Holy Spirit intervenes and comes upon all who hear! The Spirit has preceded baptism (contrast with 2:37-38).

Mutually enriched and changed, Cornelius' family becomes part of the new community and Peter remains with them for several days, accepting their table hospitality (11:3).

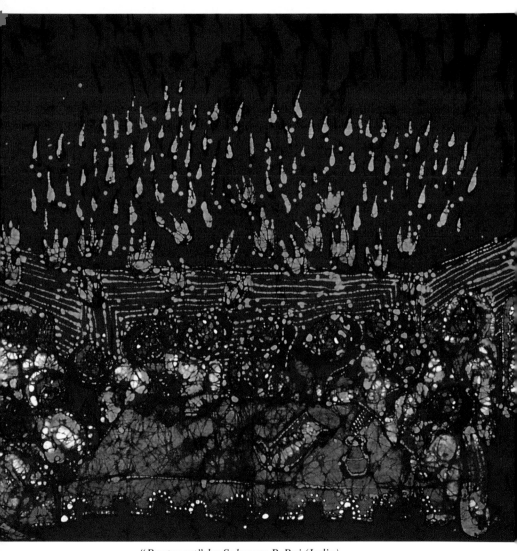

"Pentecost" by Solomon P. Raj (India)

"Pentecost" by a Westphalian master (Germany

"Philip and the Court Official" by Azariah Mbatha (South Africa), Acts 8 : 26-40

"The Soakage Pit" by Kaapa Tjampitjina (Aboriginal, Australia),
the tribal community sit together around a central site – Acts 2 : 44-45

The meeting of Peter and Cornelius led to the foundation of the Christian community in Caesarea and the expansion of Christianity in the Gentile world. When people are prepared to cross cultural frontiers in openness to the Spirit, the mission of God in Christ advances.

A story: *MUTUAL SHARING ACROSS CULTURES*

"Mission and Reconciliation" is a project started in Central America in 1992 to establish new ways of carrying out mission. Christians of different denominations (Protestants and Roman Catholics in Central America along with Presbyterians in the USA), men and women of different ages, races, educational levels and social classes are involved. The project involves people going to live in another country, with a different language and culture and different ways of living and worshipping, but undergirded by a common experience of faith and community. These people take up the challenge of leaving their own environment in order to promote a liberating process based on the gospel. The project involves work both within and outside the churches, and has led those involved to a new experience of mutual enrichment and expression in mission.

Marilie Robertson (USA) was involved for one year in mission in the northern region of the Atlantic coast of Nicaragua — a multicultural region with at least five languages — where the people live in extreme poverty. The past decade has been exceedingly painful in Central America; this pain continues as people struggle daily for survival and search for alternative ways to go forward.

Marilie said: "It was very painful *for me* to keep hearing about the history of exclusion, oblivion and neglect which this people has suffered for so many years." Nevertheless she was able to assist the Miskito women in their struggle to hold onto their cultural identity and to transform their society and even their church.

The Central Americans who went to live in the United States found themselves confronted with unexpected challenges. They came to realize that the mission of reconciliation involves addressing a great deal of misinformation and mistrust as well as helping people confront their fears about each other. They found themselves providing pastoral assistance to large numbers of refugees from Mexico, Guatemala, El Salvador, etc. — and to North American ethnic minorities as well.

This is a new mode of being in mission: a process of healing broken and discarded relationships. It is a way of facing the challenge of the gospel in mutuality across cultures.

Questions

- What religious/cultural barriers did Peter have to cross in his acceptance of Cornelius? What are some of the barriers in your context today? How does the gospel empower you to transcend them?

- What signs of acceptance did both Peter and Cornelius show to allow encounter to happen? What steps are you ready to take to accept other people, and what can you learn from their practices and culture? (Compare with how Paul acted in Athens, Acts 17.)

- "God shows no partiality, but in every nation anyone who... does what is right is acceptable to [God]" (Acts 10:34). What actions has your congregation/church taken to reach out to those in your neighbourhood who are culturally, religiously or in any other way "different"? How has this been a witness to the inclusive love of God for all people?

- What are the elements of Peter's proclamation of the gospel? How is the gospel articulated as good news in your situation?

- Peter was changed in the course of the encounter with Cornelius. Describe an experience you have had with someone of another culture or religion in which you yourself were changed.

Eternal God, whose image lies in the hearts
    of all people,
we live among peoples
    whose ways are different from ours,
    whose faiths are foreign to us,
    whose tongues are unintelligible to us.
Help us to remember
    that you love all people with your great love,
    that all religion is an attempt to respond to you,
    that the yearnings of other hearts
        are much like our own
        and are known to you.
Help us to recognize you in the words of truth,
    the things of beauty,
    the actions of love about us.
We pray through Christ,
    who is a stranger to no one land more than another,
    and to every land no less than to another.

STUDY 6

Acts 13-15

Focus: Acts 15:1-29

ONE GOSPEL, DIVERSE CULTURES, ONE COMMUNITY?

Introduction

Christians are called to share the good news of Jesus Christ with people "of all nations" (Matt. 28:19). People in different parts of the world speak different languages, see the world through different eyes and live their lives in different ways. But when people accept Jesus Christ, they become members of a new community, with a new identity and a new way of living.

This study is about what happens when diverse cultures are brought together in the name of Jesus Christ. How can those cultures encounter the gospel — and be transformed by it — without losing their distinctiveness and vitality? On the other hand, how can the distinctiveness and integrity of the Christian faith be lived in each culture?

In chapters 13-15 Luke describes how the early Christian community, which had initially focused on the Jews, continues to reach out to the Gentile world.

Luke affirms that, again, the Holy Spirit takes the initiative. After prayer and fasting, the church in Antioch hears the Spirit calling for Barnabas and Saul to be "set apart... for the work to which I have called them" (13:2): mission to the Gentiles. Henceforth, Saul is known as Paul.

Paul and Barnabas undertake a breathless itinerary of many months. A number of influential people, both Je 's and Gentiles, are brought to faith. In each city, the apostles go first to the synagogue to preach to the Jews and proselytes (13:14, 14:1). Most of the Jewish leaders in Antioch and Iconium, however, reject their message, and Paul announces: "It was necessary that the word of God should be spoken first to you. Since you reject it... we are now turning to the Gentiles" (13:46).

The response of many of the Gentiles is dramatic: great numbers believe and are baptized. This is not without cost — Paul and Barnabas are driven out of Antioch (13:50) and stoned in Iconium, and in Lystra Paul is stoned and left for dead (14:19). Nevertheless they continue to proclaim the good news and make "many disciples" in Perga, Antioch, Iconium, Lystra, Derbe and Attalia.

From Attalia, Paul and Barnabas return to Antioch, where they report how God had "opened a door of faith for the Gentiles" (14:27).

Now, in chapter 15, the church is confronted with a crisis (see also Gal. 2:1-14). What are the implications of the influx of all these Gentiles into a church which until now has been a Jewish sect? Must they become Jews and leave behind their Greek/Roman culture? Can the church live with this diversity — as one family in Christ — without the Jewish Christians dominating the Greek and Roman Christians? Has faith in Christ broken down the barriers? Can they sit at one table, share food, be recognized as full partners in one mission, without giving up their cultural distinctiveness? A great argument breaks out; it is not an easy matter to decide.

Commentary

Acts 15:1-29

1-5   Some insist that the Gentile Christians be circumcised. They are not opposed to preaching to the Gentiles: they believe that Abraham was called to be a blessing to *all* humankind. But the sign of that blessing was circumcision (Gen. 17:9-14). How could the Gentiles be blessed (saved) without circumcision?

6-7   A full council of the church is called. There is a long debate.

7-9   Peter had already learned through his experience with Cornelius (Acts 10:34) that the Holy Spirit was given without distinction to both Jews and Gentiles.

10   Peter acknowledges that the law is an unbearable yoke to Jews and Gentiles alike (cf. Paul writing in Gal. 2:15-3:29).

11   Note the contrast between this verse — which indicates that both "we" and "they" shall be saved "through the grace of the Lord Jesus" (cf. Rom. 5:1-2) — and v.1.

12-18   In the end they reach an agreement (announced by James the Lord's brother, who was the head of the church in Jerusalem — cf. Gal. 1:18) which they believe to be consistent with the scriptures. They are convinced also that this is the direction in which the Spirit is leading them in order to maintain the *koinonia* (communion, common sharing in the Spirit).

19-29   A way is found to include the Gentiles without first making them Jews, and to include them without giving offence to the Jewish Christians — a way of maintaining the unity of the church while respecting cultural differences.

The council writes a letter and appoints two senior church leaders to go with Paul and Barnabas to convey their decision to the Gentile Christians. The delegation and the council's decision are received with joy.

Stories: *MISSION IN UNITY?*

• The gospel was first brought to Russia in AD 988. Since then the Russian Orthodox Church has grown to a membership of more than 100 million. Baptist witness in Russia was introduced in the mid-nineteenth century, and Baptists now number more than 85,000. Since the end of communist rule, thousands of missionaries and evangelists have moved into Central and Eastern Europe and the former USSR. Many have established their own churches, disregarding the existing Orthodox, Baptist and other denominations — indeed often attracting members of those denominations by offering gifts and services and other "unworthy means".
• In Sydney, Australia, there are 25,000 Korean-Australians. They have formed over 70 congregations, many of which are congregations of the Uniting Church in Australia. The Uniting Church considers that it has tried hard to show hospitality. Yet for reasons of language and culture the Korean congregations have felt themselves to be marginalized and oppressed. They have moved to establish their own presbytery.
• Canada and the United States of America have received succeeding waves of immigrants. Since the turn of the century millions of people, many of them victims of oppression and persecution in their native lands, have taken refuge there. Lutherans from the

Scandinavian countries, Orthodox from Armenia and Russia, Roman Catholics from Poland and Ireland, and many others, quickly built churches as centres of worship, spiritual and social support and cultural preservation — outposts of their churches in faraway lands. Today these families of churches, due to their different ethnic backgrounds and traditions, find it difficult to express their unity in any visible way.

Questions

- It might have been easier for Paul and Barnabas to set up a separate church of Gentile Christians. Why did they consider it so important for the Gentile and Jewish Christians to remain together in the one church?

- In your congregation/parish, are people all of one race/class/culture, or of several? Do they all have the same first language? How does your church reflect the diversity of its worshippers in its liturgy, art, structures and the priorities for its life and ministries?

- Before the council met in Jerusalem both parties held to positions which they considered to be non-negotiable. Yet by studying the scriptures and listening to the Spirit they found a way (even though the circumcision requirement had stood for many centuries). What are the issues dividing Christians in your context today? Identify ways in which Christians may recognize each other's gifts and experiences and overcome such divisions.

- In your country can you name any situation in which one religion/culture imposes on or oppresses another? What form does that imposition take? How might the gospel become a liberating and transforming power in that situation?

God, you made the world and everything in it;
    you created the human race of one stock
    and gave us the earth for our possession.

We have been divisive in our thinking,
    in our speech, in our actions;
we have classified and imprisoned one another;
we have fenced each other out by hatred and prejudice.

Break down the walls that separate us
and unite us in a single body.

God, you mean us to be a single people,
    ruled by peace, feasting in freedom,
    freed from injustice, truly human, men and women,
    responsible and responsive in the life we lead,
    the love we share, the relationships we create.

We need ever-new insights into the truth,
    awareness of your will for all humanity,
    courage to do what is right
        even when it is not allowed,
    persistence in undermining unjust structures
        until they crumble into dust,
    grace to exercise a ministry of reconciliation.

Break down the walls that separate us
and unite us in a single body.

Acts 16-17

Focus: Acts 16:11-24

THE GOSPEL TRANSFORMS RELATIONSHIPS

Introduction

Chapter 16 marks a major transition in the progress of the gospel in two ways. First, the scene shifts from the predominantly Jewish and eastern Mediterranean world to mainland Europe and the encounter with various expressions of Roman culture. Second, Paul and Timothy (his chosen co-worker, whom Paul had had circumcised to minimize offence to potential Jewish hearers) share the decisions of the Council of Jerusalem "from town to town" (16:4) — symbolic of both continuity and change.

The gospel interacts with cultures and contexts in a variety of ways. It can neither be yoked to nor contained within any particular cultural experience.

Compelled by the Spirit (16:7-10), Paul changes his travel plans and proceeds to Macedonia, a centre of Roman culture and rule. With Silas and others he reaches Philippi, a leading city of the area, where they meet with women who had gathered by the river for prayer. Lydia, a dealer in purple cloth, is baptized, and a slave girl is freed from a "spirit of divination".

Paul and his friends are branded as "disturbing" elements (16:20), people who have been "turning the world upside down" (17:6). Public unrest is stirred up in Philippi, Thessalonica and Beroea. In Philippi, Paul and Silas are flogged and imprisoned (16:23) and eventually asked to leave (16:39). In Beroea, the believers send Paul away for his own protection (17:14).

Paul is then taken to Athens, where the dramatic encounter between the message of Christ and the wisdom of the Greeks takes place. At the Areopagus Paul is invited to present "this new teaching" (17:19). When Paul speaks of the resurrection of the dead, there are different reactions: some scoff, others want to know more, and still others "joined him and became believers" (16:32-33).

The gospel interacts with each specific cultural context in creative ways. It affirms some elements of each culture and finds roots therein. The gospel also critiques elements of each culture, taking an uncompromising stand on issues of liberation, justice and human dignity, and promising fullness of life in Christ for all. Sometimes cultures and traditions are used to subjugate or exploit particular sections of society in the name of order and harmony. What then is the response of the gospel as it encounters oppressive, exploitative relationships that are legitimized in the name of culture?

In Acts 16 are presented the stories of two women whose contact with the gospel results in a stronger assertion of life. The coming of the gospel brings them, respectively, new relationships and freedom from bondage. (The latter story may take on fresh relevance in the contemporary context, with the increasing phenomenon of spiritism as well as the exploitation of children and young women.)

Commentary

Acts 16:11-15

12-14   In Philippi, Paul's first encounter is with a group of women who have met for prayer "outside the gate". Lydia listens to the gospel eagerly and is later baptized, along with her household. This encounter on the banks of the river outside the city marks the beginning of a transformed fellowship which becomes a significant centre of Christianity in the early church (cf. Phil. 1:1).

15   After she is baptized, Lydia invites Paul, Silas and Timothy to stay in her house. After their imprisonment and miraculous release from prison, they go back to Lydia's home and encourage the small community of "brothers and sisters" (16:40) which had been brought into being by the transforming power of the gospel. Does not the gospel often effect new patterns of relationships between women and men and with strangers, binding them into a new community of love?

Faithfulness to God is expressed in hospitality to the saints (2 Cor. 8:3-5). Wealthy disciples were expected to share their wealth (Acts 2:44-45, 4:32-35); Lydia uses hers to provide hospitality. Note that the church in Philippi was the object of Paul's special love; it was the only one from which he later received gifts (cf. Phil. 4:15-16).

Acts 16:16-24

16   A young slave girl is liberated by the power of the gospel from two kinds of bondage: bondage to a "spirit of divination", and bondage to a syndicate of owners. It is a story of the gospel challenging the organized economic exploitation of defenceless people.

17   The girl, like those possessed by demons in the gospels (Mark 3:11, Luke 4:41), recognizes the power of the Spirit of God in these "slaves of the Most High God", and that they have something unique to offer.

18-19   Paul casts out the spirit in the name of Jesus Christ. The same Holy Spirit, the Spirit of the risen Lord, is at work in the apostles. These are the "greater works than these" that Jesus promised the disciples would do (John 14:12) — "greater" because they are done in many places. The gospel challenges and transforms structures of bondage.

20-21   The real issue is not what Paul and Silas believe but the ethics they practise and the transforming effect of the gospel they announce. The gospel is thus not simply a set of propositions but rather a way of life — and this way of life is seen as subversive to the life of the Romans.

God offers us freedom
   through our Lord Jesus Christ.
For the spirit of life in Christ Jesus
   has set us free from the law of sin and death.
For we did not receive the spirit of slavery
   to fall back into fear;
but we have received the spirit
   of the children of God.

A story: *A STRUGGLE FOR JUSTICE AND DIGNITY*

Dalits are the despised, oppressed, untouchable people outside the Indian caste system. They are made and kept poor, exploited by the dominant sections of the society. Religious and cultural symbols and structures legitimate this systemic injustice. Dalits are made to believe that their predicament is a result of their past sins and that the only way to liberate themselves is by doing their own caste duties honestly and diligently.

There have been a number of resistance movements against this structural violence in the history of supposedly "non-violent" Indian society. Since the arrival of the missionaries in the nineteenth century, the witness to the gospel furthered the process of the mass awakening of the dalits. The church offered them the possibility of gaining a new dignified identity, liberation from hopeless situations of misery and suffering, and opportunities for education and gainful employment. Dalits in some parts of the country joined the church in large numbers. Supporters of the caste system turned hostile to the proclamation of the gospel. At the same time, upper-caste Christians resented the dalits' entry and the new dalit image that the Indian church was gaining. In fact, the encounter of the message of the gospel with Indian society effected a number of significant reforms.

But many of the churches in India today seem to have lost this radical, liberative witness and have opted for forms of evangelism which leave oppressive power structures in place. Caste continues to exist and operate within the church, encouraging dominant/dependent relationships.

Empowered by the gospel, dalit Christians — together with others — are fighting for justice, equality and dignity.

Questions

- In what ways has the gospel brought women and men into a new relationship with one another in your community?

- The apostles sense the spirituality of Lydia and her companions even before they proclaim the gospel to them. In what ways are you sensitive to the Spirit at work in people prior to their response to the gospel?

- Lydia responded to the generosity of God by offering hospitality to the brothers and sisters in Christ. What could be some of the concrete implications of this for your congregation?

- What aspects of your culture legitimate and perpetuate bondages? What are some of the contemporary bondages for women — particularly young women — in your context? What is the liberating power of the gospel in such situations?

- How does your church act in solidarity with marginalized and oppressed people?

O God, through your Word, remind us
that the final power is life and not death
   reconciliation and not oppression
   justice and not servitude
   love and not fear
   dignity and not shame
   healing and not tearing
   loving care and not self-serving carelessness
   generosity and not meanness
   God-with-us and not lonely abandonment
   Spirit-in-me and not cringing weakness.
God whose Word became human and lived among us,
teach us to trust ourselves without fear,
you whose Word is stronger than any other power,
and more trustworthy than any other word.

"WE COMMIT OURSELVES..."

Sisters and brothers,
the call still comes to us:
"Whom will I send? Who will go for me?"
What will our answer be?

We will go. Send us.
Together we will carry the gospel.
Together we will bear our small lights
into the church and into the world.
For there are not other hands but our hands
* to carry them.*
We are always the broken body
but in Christ we are made whole.

In great thanksgiving
we celebrate the riches of our diversity
as the living signs
of the imagination of God.

We commit ourselves
to receive from each other special gifts
as we are led in the power of the Holy Spirit
towards abundant life.

Acknowledgments

We wish to thank all those who have granted permission for the use of prayers and illustrations in this book. We have made every effort to trace and identify them correctly and to secure all the necessary permissions for reprinting. If we have erred in any way in the acknowledgments, or have unwittingly infringed any copyright, we apologize sincerely. We would be glad to make the necessary corrections in subsequent editions of this book.

Bible studies

The basic material for the Bible studies was prepared by a group of ten persons who met in Geneva in April 1995: the Rev. Dr John Brown (Australia), the Rev. M. Deenabandhu (India), Deacon Michael Findikyan (USA/Italy), Archimandrite Iannuary Ivliev (Russia), the Rev. Dr Mac Charles Jones (USA), the Rev. Martha Mumbi Ngugi (Kenya), Ms Najla Abousawan Kassab (Lebanon), Prof. Dr Milton Schwantes (Brazil) and the Rev. Alison White (UK). The stories included in each study were told by the participants in that meeting. The final editorial and other work on the studies was done by Unit II staff — Sr Monica Cooney smsm, the Rev. Dr Christopher Duraisingh and Ms Dawn Ross — assisted by Dr Brown.

Illustrations

1. "Pentecost", batik by Solomon P. Raj, from *Living Flame and Springing Fountain: Batiks and Meditations* by Solomon Raj, © the author, published by ISPCK, Delhi, India, 1993, p.40.

2. "Philip and the Court Official", linocut by Azariah Mbatha, South Africa, photo by H. Helf, from *Christliche Kunst in Afrika* by J.F. Thiel & H. Helf, © Dietrich Reimer Verlag, Berlin, and Haus Völker und Kulturen, St Augustin, 1984, p.282.

3. "Pentecost", painting by a Westphalian master, ca. 1380.

4. "The Soakage Pit", by Kaapa Tjampitjina, from *The Bible through Asian Eyes* by Masao Takenaka and Ron O'Grady, © 1991 Asian Christian Art Association, Japan, published by Pace Publishers, New Zealand, p.169.

Prayers

Page vi: (Orthodox) Vespers of Pentecost, in *The Oxford Book of Prayer*, ed. George Appleton, Oxford, Oxford University Press, 1987, p.207.

Pages viii and 42: "A Liturgy of Commitment", in *International Review of Mission*, vol. LXXXIV, nos 332/333, January-April 1995, pp.153,156-57.

Page 5, 9, 13: Staff editorial team, using material adapted from a variety of sources.

Page 17: From *Love Poured Out: Mission Prayer Handbook 1994*, Uniting Church in Australia, National Commission for Mission, p.55.

Page 18: Extract from "Come, Holy Spirit, renew the whole creation, send the wind and flame", by Dorothy McRae-McMahon, Uniting Church in Australia, © the author, in *In Spirit and In Truth: A Worship Book*, prepared for the WCC's seventh assembly in Canberra, WCC Publications, Geneva, Switzerland, 1991, p.23.

Page 22: From *Your Will Be Done – Notes on an "Unfinished Agenda". Mission Prayer Handbook 1989,* Uniting Church in Australia, National Commission for Mission, p.33.

Pages 25 and 41: From *Images of God: Mission Prayer Handbook 1991,* Uniting Church in Australia, National Commission for Mission, pp.48 and 52.

Page 31: Based on a prayer by Robert H. Adams Jr, *A Traveller's Prayer Book*, Nashville, TN, The Upper Room, adapted as it appeared in *Jesus Christ — The Life of the World: A Worship Book*, prepared for the WCC's sixth assembly in Vancouver, WCC Publications, Geneva, Switzerland, 1983, p.97.

Page 36: Extract from "Lord, you made the world and everything in it", in *Let's Worship*, worship book for the WCC's fifth assembly in Nairobi, *Risk*, vol. 11, nos 2-3, 1975, pp.43-45.

Page 39: Adapted from "Sisters and brothers we have come together", in *In Spirit and In Truth: A Worship Book*, WCC Publications, Geneva, Switzerland, 1991, p.7.